Buss

The Smart Girl's Guide to Your Destiny

Marina Crook

Piccadilly Press • London

For Katy, Caroline, Hamish and Harry.
May your destinies be wonderful.

First published in Great Britain in 2001
by Piccadilly Press Ltd.,
5 Castle Road, London NW1 8PR

Photoypeset from the author's disc
in 10.5 Futura Book

A catalogue record for this book
is available from the British Library

ISBN: 1 85340 692 9 (paperback)

3 5 7 9 10 8 6 4 2

Printed and bound in Great Britain by Bookmarque Ltd.

Design by Louise Millar
Picture research by Caroline Hunter

CONTENTS

INTRODUCTION

How many times have you wondered what job you'll have? How often do you daydream about when you're going to fall in love? How regularly do you think about the future?

Well, if you're a normal person, the answer is a lot of the time. Thinking about what's in store is natural and even the most cynical of us can't help peeking at our horoscopes to find a clue about what's about to happen.

Looking into your destiny is nothing new. Thousands of years ago people used methods, similar to those used now, to try to discover what the future held. They believed that it gave them power, and even if their insight caused them to act and then determine their future, that made them even stronger.

Now there's no way that every aspect of your

future can be found in the next seventeen chapters, but this book will help you find out about yourself. And knowing yourself now will help you know yourself in time to come. *The Smart Girl's Guide to Your Destiny* is packed with divinatory tools – techniques like I Ching, horoscopes and graphology that are used to help predict. They'll help you learn more about what's going to happen to you and your relationships with your friends, family and boys! The tools will help you understand your intuition better and point you in the direction of possibilities. Then it's up to you to make those possibilities come true. Each chapter explains why a particular way of predicting is right for each area of your life. It then tells you how to use it. To peek into your destiny doesn't take money or complicated processes. All you'll need is your head and your heart, and occasionally a pen or pack of playing cards.

The most important thing to remember when you're using *The Smart Girl's Guide to Your Destiny*, is that it can't hold all the answers to life. Only you can do that. But what it can do is stir up all your senses into exploring what you really want and what you're capable of achieving. And it can help make your future start sooner rather than later.

You can work your way through the book in three ways:

1 Search the contents pages to find the chapter that interests you most. For example, if you are worried about how your relationship with your parents is going, choose a chapter that can help you gain insight into this.

2 Find the divinatory tool that most appeals to you. If you're an astrology freak, turn straight to those pages and slowly try out the divinatory tools at your leisure.

3 Start at the beginning and use each section to try and learn more about yourself, your interaction with your friends and family and then with boys. By the time you come to the end of the book, you won't have your future mapped out, but you will have a clearer idea of where you're going and you'll know yourself better – and you'll have had lots of fun.

Every chapter can be done with a friend, if you take it in turns.

So now relax, clear your mind, and prepare to peek into your destiny. And remember, always go with your instincts and be true to yourself.

Chapter 1

THE GODDESS THEORY

Your whole future's ahead of you, and fate might have lots in store. But don't think that what happens to you is altogether out of your control. The most important thing to understand about your destiny is that it's going to be what you make of it. If numerology tells you that you've got great communication skills, it doesn't mean that you're going to miraculously land a TV presenter's job. Your destiny happens when you find out about yourself and use what you learn.

You are a Goddess. In the same way that the

Greek Goddess, Aphrodite, had the power of love, you have your own powers. All you have to do is work out what they are, and learn how to use them. Once you know your strengths, you can use them to build your future the way you want it.

WHAT'S YOUR GODDESS POWER?

To find out what your inner female strength is, answer the following questions and collect points as you go:

1 Are you:

a Sporty?	10
b Arty?	5
c Academic?	1

2 What's your ideal day out?

a Shopping	10
b Bowling with mates	5
c Walking in the country with a friend	1

3 What do you value most?

a Jewellery	1
b CDs	10
c Clothes	5

4 Are you:

a Loud? 10

b Shy? 1

c A bit of both? 5

5 Which of these jobs would you most like to do?

a Teacher 1

b Singer 10

c Business woman 5

5–20 points
You're a Goddess of Calm

Your strengths lie in your cautious, calm nature. You impress people by taking the back seat in a conversation then chipping in an intelligent, thoughtful or witty comment. Being quiet makes you mysterious and intriguing – don't assume it's a fault.

21–35 points
You're a Goddess of Cool

Your strengths lie in your practical, down-to-earth nature. You're a trusted friend who will always be turned to. You don't need frivolous things to make you happy. People love you because you're real.

35 points and over
You're a Goddess of Wild

Your strengths lie in your energetic, exciting nature. The party starts with you. You embrace challenge and love new people and experiences. You're a bright light that draws people in.

Goddess Power

Now that you know what sort of Goddess you are, you can find out what to do to use your strengths and push your destiny along. Remember your title and look out for tips throughout the book.

Chapter 2

WHERE YOU'RE AT

Before you can begin to explore what's going to happen in the future, you have to understand what's happening now. Everything we do helps shape the person we are. Being human, we're pretty rubbish at recognising our strengths and weaknesses. If we're brilliant at maths we play it down because we don't want to look like a big-head. If we've been bitchy, we try to hide it because we don't want people to think we're horrible. The only way to be really honest with yourself and find out about yourself is to ask yourself some questions. To find out where you're at in life, try the flow chart on the next page.

START
Are you the leader of your gang?

NO → Do you have more than one best friend?

YES ↓

Do your friends copy you?

NO →

NO ↓

Do you wake up feeling worried?

NO

YES

YES ↓

Are you on top of your schoolwork?

YES → Do your friends help you with your homework?

YES

NO ↓

Do you enjoy being top of the class?

NO → Do you have interests outside school?

YES ↓

Are you more popular than most?

NO →

YES ↓

NO → Do you have to work hard at everything?

YES ↓

In your group have you had the most snogs?

NO → Do boys tell you that they fancy your mates?

YES →

NO ↓

YES ↓

TYPE A

TYPE B

14

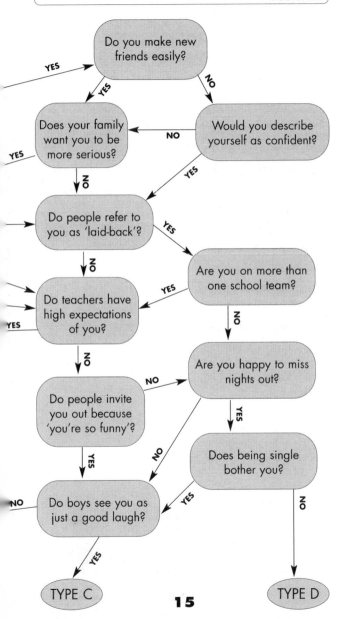

YES → Do you make new friends easily?
YES ↓   NO →

Does your family want you to be more serious? ← NO ─ Would you describe yourself as confident?
YES
↓ NO   YES ↓

Do people refer to you as 'laid-back'? ── YES →
↓ NO   Are you on more than one school team?
                                          YES ←
Do teachers have high expectations of you? ← YES
YES   ↓ NO
↓ NO   Are you happy to miss nights out?
                                          NO →
Do people invite you out because 'you're so funny'?   ↓ YES
                                              Does being single bother you?
↓ YES   NO
NO ─   YES   ↓ NO
Do boys see you as just a good laugh?

↓ YES   ↓ NO
TYPE C   15   TYPE D

Type A – The achiever

You're the envy of lots of girls at school. On the face of it you appear to have everything. You pass exams without too much trouble, you've got lots of friends and you're confident enough to pull boys. You're at a stage when you should be very pleased with yourself. But being an achiever does have its drawbacks. You're likely to get complacent and might find yourself slipping behind with your schoolwork. Also, make sure you let your mates know how much you care about them.

Although no one ever expects it, you're prone to insecurity – being Miss Popular is a tough role to live up to. Don't beat yourself up, let your mates know you're only human, enjoy life and realise how lucky you are.

Type B – The tryer

Sometimes you can't believe just how hard you have to try to get half of what other people seem to have. Although you've got great mates and you're doing well in all areas of your life, things don't seem to come easy to you. Your friends and family love you and even your teachers realise how hard-working you are. Give yourself a break. Having to

16

strive to achieve is a good thing. When you get rewards they're so much more exciting, and everything you're putting in now will be paid back to you tenfold in years to come. Just because boys aren't queuing up to go out with you now, it doesn't mean it won't happen in the future. They like you for you, and your relationships will be meaningful.

Type C – The amuser

When you're feeling low, you think, Why doesn't anyone take me seriously? But when you're on form you love being the class clown. At the moment there are lots of things in life that you want but seem to be out of your reach. Be honest – is that someone else's fault, or have you not put enough work in yet? You excel socially but academically feel average. Don't worry, use your talents to help you achieve. You're funny and although you're not super-confident you're not scared of making a fool of yourself. By your late teens people will be jealous of you because your qualities will be noticed and your peers will be less judgemental. One thing to remember is that you'll be taken seriously if you approach people properly. Let them know that you're not joking and they'll sit up and listen.

Type D – The loner

You're quite happy with where you are at the moment, but you just wish people would let you get on with it. You tend to see life in a different way from most, and don't understand why everyone at school needs to conform to their groups. You've got your own interests and don't depend on one gang for mates. Your teachers admire your talents but don't always like your attitude. Don't let it get to you. Instead, try to see things from others' points of view but still defend your own beliefs. Because you're a loner, some girls, particularly the bitchy ones, may react nastily to you. Don't let that make you hide away, but hold your head high. You're strong and you know your own mind, and this will be invaluable to you through life. When it comes to boys, you know you're not bothered about attracting the cutest boy in school, so chill out and wait for the right lad for you!

Tip for all types of Goddess

Don't ever try to be someone you're not: people will see through you straight away. To be happy, be true to you.

Chapter 3

COULD YOU BE SUCCESSFUL?

Graphology

Deep down we all want to achieve. Some of us just want to find love and happiness, but some of us really want to succeed in a career or even become famous too. But being successful or famous takes a lot of hard work and some fundamental talents. So have you got what it takes? It's impossible to work out what you're going to achieve just yet, but it is possible to find out if you've some of the ingredients needed to make an amazing career for yourself or even become a star. And those answers might be found in graphology.

What is graphology?

Graphology is the study of handwriting.

How does it work?

Everything from the slant of your letters, to the way you dot your 'i's and cross your 't's says something about your personality.

What can it tell you about yourself?

Graphology can tell you about all different areas of your life, but it's particularly relevant when it comes to finding out about career and fame potential. There are so many clues in the way that we present ourselves in a signature alone, that can point towards whether we've got what it takes, or if we have the desire for a successful future.

Signing up for success

Each aspect of your handwriting style gives a hint about you and about your talents.

Grab a piece of paper and a pen that you feel most comfortable writing with, then write a random sentence of at least eight words.

Now look at the sentence and analyse your writing using the following guide.

20

SIZE

The size of your handwriting suggests how you feel about yourself.

Large

What that says about you: You're ambitious, enthusiastic, creative, sociable and confident.

What that says about you and success or fame: You'd be happy to confidently seek out stardom. You'd put yourself in the right scenarios to become famous.

Medium

What that says about you: You're conventional, happy, practical and a good worker.

What that says about you and success or fame: You don't want success so much that you'd be prepared to lose anything for it. If it happened, it wouldn't change your personality.

Small

What that says about you: You need your own space, you're cautious, observant, realistic and mathematical.

THE SMART GIRL'S GUIDE TO **YOUR DESTINY**

What that says about you and success or fame: You'd only become successful because of your passion for what your hobby is. If you did become a star, you'd turn your back on fame after a short time.

SPACING

The space we leave between each word tells us how we communicate with people, which is really important if you want a big career.

Wide spaces

What that says about you: You're into music, you're secretive and need to keep people at arm's length.

What that says about you and success or fame: You're more likely to be a key player but not be in the limelight. Your creativity suggests a career in the media, but maybe behind the scenes, for example a theatre stage manager, a TV researcher, or work in publishing. You'd be quite happy to see your project working without needing to get the glory.

Narrow spacing
What that says about you: You're outgoing, loud and impulsive.

What that says about you and success or fame: You'd hound people to get what you want, and you'd have no trouble getting people to notice you. In interviews you'd lap up the opportunity to express yourself.

SLANTS
The direction of the slant of your handwriting can also say a lot about you.

Slanting to the right
What that says about you: You're sociable, enterprising, enthusiastic and great at meeting new people.

What that says about you and success or fame: You'd feel confident walking into a record company or agent's office and selling yourself.

Slanting to the left
What that says about you: You're cautious, practical and like doing things alone.

23

What that says about you and success or fame: You'd sooner be noticed almost by accident because of your talent, than sell yourself to get on to a manager role or make it as a celeb.

Straight up

What that says about you: You're a team player who's confident and keen.

What that says about you and success or fame: You'd sooner reach your goals with a group of friends: you'd have more confidence with the support of your closest people.

STYLE

The touches you add to the original way you were taught to write at school reflect your flamboyance and therefore your chances of being noticed.

Sweeping tails on 'y's or 'g's

What that says about you: You're creative and like to stand out for being different.

What that says about you and success or fame: You could be spotted as having something fresh or new to bring to a career.

Lots of loops; circles rather than dots over 'i's

What that says about you: You're trying a bit too hard.

What that says about you and success or fame: You'll be noticed more for what you pick up from other people.

Very neat

What that says about you: You're a conformer who likes to know exactly what's happening.

What that says about you and success or fame: You'd be perfect in a producing type of role, where you organise people or events. Your neatness makes you an ideal candidate for lots of successful careers.

Very messy

What that says about you: You're artistic and look at the world in an unusual way.

What that says about you and success or fame: You might have the talent, but you wouldn't want to do as you were told or put in the hard work. You'd be happier not being the boss or taking a leading role.

Change your style

If you really want to push your destiny a different way from where it seems to be going, altering the way you write can help do that.

- It's sad that people are so vain, but if you start writing more in the style of the person you want to impress, they will subconsciously warm to you.

- If your handwriting needs to be more disciplined to get on, work at it and take your time. The effort put in will help you anyway, by teaching you about hard work – very important if you're going to be the next Anita Roddick (the woman who started The Body Shop) or the next Posh Spice.

- If you think you're a bit uptight and want to be more relaxed all round, start with your handwriting. Drop in unnecessary swirls and see if they make you feel liberated or silly!

Tips for finding success

- Start thinking about what you're really interested in now and look into getting work experience in that area.

- Grab any opportunity that comes along. If

you're interested in publishing, enter writing competitions. If you want to be an actor and someone's filming in your town, hang around and try to be an extra.

- Think about what your skills are and use them. If you sound like a screeching cat but you're a great sports person, don't aim to be a singer, but put your energies into getting into the Olympics.
- Get as many papers and mags about the career you're interested in as you can find.
- Take up lots of hobbies that can help develop your skills.
- Speak to anybody who knows about the career you're interested in to find out if it's something you're really right for.

Tip for Goddesses of Calm
Never let others push you into roles you're not comfortable with.

Chapter 4

WILL YOU GET WHAT YOU WANT?

Luck Tables & Geomancy

THE LUCK TABLE

Sometimes good old-fashioned luck is the only thing you need to fulfill your destiny. But even when that's the case, using your Goddess power can help you make luck swing your way. To find out more use a luck table.

What is a luck table?

A luck table is a simple chart that works in the

same way as a lucky eight ball. It lets you know possible outcomes to questions spinning around your mind. It also helps you to think about some of the stuff lying around in your subconscious.

How does it work?

Think carefully about a question you want an answer to. Close your eyes, then toss a five pence coin on to the luck table at least five times. If the majority of the coin lands on a square, what that square says is your answer. If the coin lands between two squares, toss again. If the coin lands between three or four squares, the table is telling you that it's too early to discover that answer yet. Try again another day.

What does it say about you?

The luck table helps you find out what's really important to you. The order in which the questions pop into your head is a big clue.

What to do.

Ask up to six questions at any one time. Think hard then ask very specific things, e.g. Will he notice me tomorrow? Can I get better at English? Should I join the drama club?

Yes. But put in more effort.	No. But in time.	If you believe in yourself.
Yes. But do you really want that?	Others are in the way now.	If you feel really positive.
You're not ready.	Yes, the time is right.	Yes, if you make a plan.
Your friends can help you.	Don't give up hope.	Follow your instincts.

Will you be happy or rich?

Now that you've thought about how lucky you're going to be, it's quite fun to think about being rich!

There are lots of old beliefs about being lucky with money, through money e.g 'Find a penny, pick it up.' In a similar way to using the luck table, you can ask coins questions about whether or not you'll be wealthy. One prediction tool is money spinning.

What is money spinning?

Money spinning is simply flicking a coin while asking it a question. Money spinning is purely based on luck – it's one of the divinatory tools that work on the idea that it might be a lucky day – you know, one of those days when the bus comes on time and you find a pound in the street. If it's a lucky day, then it's a good one to be thinking about your finances.

How does it work?

First choose heads or tails; both are as lucky as each other. Then start flicking your coin with one hand, catch it in the same one and turn it over on to the back of the other hand to reveal a head or a tail. Ask very specific questions like you did with the luck table, e.g. Will I be richer in six months' time? Will I get a Saturday job? or Will I have enough money to buy a new pair of Nikes?

What can it tell you about yourself?

It'll make you think about how important money is to you.

Money spinning

Keep flicking and asking questions until you flick wrongly (i.e. if you've been calling heads and it comes out tails, stop) as this might be suggesting that your financial luck is running out for today. And don't worry if you don't flick right at all, it in no way means that you'll never have a penny.

Money superstitions

Old wives' tales they might be, but these are supposed to mean you're coming into cash:

- An itch on your right palm or ankle.
- Finding a small red spider.
- Finding a feather.

WILL YOU BE HAPPY?
– GEOMANCY

You might have all the luck in the world, and you

might even become a millionaire, but will all this make you happy? One fun way to try to predict happiness is to use geomancy.

What is geomancy?

Geomancy used to mean divination using earth. In the old days people used to look at the way that sand or dirt fell through their hands on to a surface to see signs of what was in store. Today there are different methods of using it, but all look at the shapes cast.

How does it work?

There are two ways you can use geomancy to find out if you might be happy. The first is to get some sand (at least four handfuls) and lay it on a tray. You then close your eyes and, holding a stick or pencil, relax and let the pointer move for a few seconds, while asking questions, till you get some outline in the sand. The second, and easiest, is to get a piece of paper and a pencil and blindfold yourself, or close your eyes or sit in a darkened room. Again you let the pencil flow as you ask yourself questions.

What can it tell you about yourself?

Geomancy reads the way that your body instinctively responds to questions, so it's a bit like having a peek at what your subconscious is saying.

How to do it

Completely relax, using whichever method suits you best, and sit with your wrist resting on the edge of a tray or table, so that you're less in control. The darkness will mean that you have little idea of what you're doing. Then ask yourself a question. Be as specific as possible, e.g. Will I smile more than ten times a day? Could I spring out of bed in the morning? Should I call him? In response to this question you're hoping to see a letter type of mark, but if you are getting a shape that might mean something else, use your own interpretation.

Then ask other specific questions about what might make you happy, looking at the mark/sign for each. (If you get a letter shape here, try again till you get something resembling a more relevant sign.)

Ask yourself at least six questions, although the amount is not that important.

Key

The closest shapes or letters to the ones below will show the following meanings:

Y – Yes

M – Maybe

N – No

Big cross – Love

A pointed shape, like a triangle – Great work prospects

A square shape – Good home life

A line that ends sharply (i.e. is broken off) – Someone is coming into your life

Tip for Goddesses of Wild

Don't expect all your friends to strive for what you want. You'll be frustrated and they'll feel alienated.

Chapter 5

YOUR
FIVE YEARS
AHEAD

Astrology

We all are intrigued about what's round the corner, whether it's an A in science, a new pair of jeans, a fight, or a boy, but it's harder to think about what's going to be going on over the next five years. It's impossible to imagine our lives changing very much, but using what we know about ourselves and a little astrology, we can make some educated guesses.

What is astrology?

Astrology is the study of what appear to be coincidences between the things happening on earth and the positions of the Sun, Moon and eight planets (they're often known as stars). Basically, it was thought that what we could see in the sky had an effect on our lives on earth. Nowadays the view is that events coincide with a particular pattern of the stars. The twelve signs of the zodiac are thirty-degree arcs that the sun appears to go through as the earth moves round it. The characteristics of each sign have been built up from years of recording what happened when the sun was in that sign.

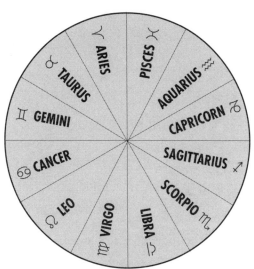

How does it work?

Using a birth chart, which is a diagram showing the positions of the Sun, Moon and the planets at the time of a person's birth, astrologers compare these positions with the movements of the planets and the Moon. They then make predictions from the trends they find.

What can it tell you about yourself?

Astrology tells you that you might have certain characteristics. It's up to you to interpret that information how you will. For example, Aries are passionate – you can take this to mean that you're likely to punch someone if they insult your boyfriend, or that you sweetly care for him so much that you'll always protect him.

♈ ARIES

March 21 – April 20
Flower – Nasturtium
Animal – Tiger
Stone – Ruby
Colours – Bright reds

You're a strong individual with loads of energy, who likes taking risks. So over the next couple of years you're likely to run off to a college miles away from home. You're also determined and logical, so although you might find yourself studying something out of the ordinary, you'll approach it in the same way you approach your maths homework. You're also a sentimental and emotional person who has very close ties with family and one or two friends. These relationships will only get better with time, but within three years you'll find that people who are in your gang, but who are not your closest mates, probably won't be around. But that will be your choice. Being alone doesn't bother Aries girls, and as soon as you can persuade your parents you'll be off on a solo expedition.

Aries are very passionate, physical, and very faithful. Expect to have a few long-term big loves over the next five years. You'll enjoy amazingly loving, happy times, but you'll also feel let down occasionally. Aries girls always give more than their partners.

♉ **TAURUS**
April 21 – May 21
Flower – Carnation
Animal – Cat
Stone – Jade

Colours – Green, cream

You're determined and devoted to whatever it is you do, so although work's a struggle at the moment, in the next five years it'll come more easily and you'll reach your goals. You like to fit in, so it's likely you'll choose a job or college maybe for comfort rather than excitement, more than likely with friends you know now.

You love your gang and they know they can turn to you whenever they're in trouble. There's no reason to expect that your social group will alter much over the next five years. But be careful. If you do have a fall-out with a close mate, you're likely to keep your anger bottled up – even for a year! This could be a problem, because at some point you'll explode and your mate might not be able ever to forgive this outburst.

Your family life is very close, but expect some big rows over the next two or three years. Taureans are stubborn and the only way to avoid Mum or Dad shouting is to force yourself to be flexible.

Taurus girls get on with all different sorts of boys really well, so over the next couple of years you'll enjoy fun short-term flings. But expect to find your soul mate within five years and when that

40

happens you'll have an incredible time. When Taurus girls love, they love with their whole heart, and appreciate what a great boy they've found.

♊ GEMINI

May 21 – June 21
Flower – Larkspur
Animal – Monkey
Stone – Tiger's eye
Colours – Black and white together, sharp yellow

Geminis are up for a laugh and don't take anything seriously. You're also really spontaneous and love having ten projects going on at once. This is fine at first but you're not Supergirl and will find in the next couple of years that you struggle to juggle everything. Gemini girls chop and change so expect to change your mind regularly about what you want to do. Your saving grace is that you're such a charmer you get away with almost anything. People trust you and look up to you, so expect a leadership role in the next two years. Your communication skills will eventually land you a brilliant job in later life.

You're Miss Popular – everyone wants to be your

41

friend. Your circle of mates will just get bigger and bigger, and in the next five years you'll be partying non-stop, and invited everywhere.

Geminis are destined to search for real love for years. To find Mr Right you'll play the numbers game, dating and dumping loads of poor unsuspecting lads till your dream boy comes along. But you will have fun along the way, and after a couple of years when you do find Mr Right, you'll grab him, hold him tight, and do your best not to let him go.

♋ CANCER
June 22 – July 22
Flower – Convolvulus
Animal – Crab
Stone – Moonstone
Colours – Pastels, silver

You're a very sensitive person, which means that you are generous, tolerant and compassionate, but it also means that you're petrified of being hurt. This can cause problems for Cancer girls, because instead of getting out there and doing it, you're likely to hide away. By not taking risks you might be stopping yourself from going for the goal you really want. Cancer girls are logical and safe. You'll do well in your exams and in college applications because you are aware of what you're good at.

Cancer girls are maternal at any age, so you probably already find that you're the one who takes care of your mates and your brothers and sisters. You make people very happy and they know that they can always depend on you, although they might all try to get you to be a bit more impulsive over the next couple of years.

Because Cancer is the sensitive sign, sadly you're going to go through some love traumas. But don't let them get to you. One day you'll be truly adored. You'll search for a boy who can take care of you, once you find him you'll love him completely.

♌ LEO
July 23 – August 23
Flower – Marigold
Animal – Lion
Stone – Citrine
Colours – Orange, gold

Leo girls are natural leaders, so you're already making a big impact at school. You're probably doing well in your favourite subjects and are already quite sure of what you want later on. Leos have the tendency to let people know what they're good at. Some might think you're vain, but it's good to be a self-publicist. You're spontaneous, lively and love excitement, so expect the unexpected in the next five years. But with Leos' hard work ethic, you'll eventually achieve great things.

At home you're proud of your bedroom which is great for your parents but not so good for your little brother or sister if they dare invade your space. Most arguments will be about this. Leos hate apologising, which might cause troubles with your parents too. In a couple of years' time they won't find this as hard, but right now it'll cause problems.

Leo girls have to fight the boys off, so expect a lot of dating in the near future. They also are happy to keep boys as friends when they break up. But remember to be sensitive to them – just because you can handle it, it doesn't mean they can. You won't settle for years yet, and when you do you'll have high demands, but once they are achieved you'll find complete happiness.

♍ **VIRGO**
August 24 – September 23
Flower – Clover

Animal – Magpie
Stone – Agate
Colours – Green, light brown

You're gentle, self-analytical and shy. Virgo girls will always do well in education and in work because they always strive to do their best. You're happier taking a back seat, and you're super organised, so it's very likely that you'll end up being the assistant to a highly successful person.

You're close to your family, you need them and you need regular attention. If everything's happy at home, you'll have lovely couple of secure years, but if any of your family criticise or tease you, you're going to be miserable. You're sometimes a bit too sensitive, not just with your family but with everyone.

You're very choosy about your mates, and some people might think of you as a bit of a snob, but you just know what and who you like. Expect a bumpy but exciting love life in the next two to three years. Virgo girls are notorious for throwing themselves into love and romance, but you're fussy. If you haven't found the right lad in the next four years you'll feel very low and think that there are no single boys left in the world. Don't panic – he will turn up – just use your Virgo charm to pull him.

♎ LIBRA

September 24 – October 23
Flower – Orchid
Animal – Dove
Stone – Opal
Colours – Pink, blue

You're friendly, caring and attentive, and only really happy when you're with other people. Also, being the sign of scales, you're brilliant at weighing things up. In the next few years this will come in very handy. You'll make excellent choices at school and you'll be the one in your gang who'll sort out all the arguments. Libran girls don't like confrontation, which can be a good thing. You're likely to get on with everyone you need to to help you get into college or find the right job for you.

You're very dependent on your friends and if you don't see them for a bit you can actually get quite upset. Your next few years with them will be the basis for great long-term friendships. Basically those girls will never forget your good advice and how many times you offered your shoulder to cry on.

When it comes to loving someone, Libran girls are the best. You're attentive and gentle and you'll give him everything. But you're wise about love. For the next few years you'll date a few different boys and get to know yourself first.

♏ SCORPIO
October 24 – November 22
Flower – Anemone
Animal – Falcon
Stone – Jasper
Colours – Dark red, black

You've got a very strong character. People know you're trustworthy and able to get what you want in life. You're a bit of a leader and can be quite domineering. You've probably already got a game plan for the next three years, even if it's only subconscious, and you're doing everything you can now, to get what you want from school. You'll use your cunning to get teachers on your side: people want to help you. Work is your passion and it's where you show how determined you are. You don't like wasting time, so expect to have a very busy couple of years with outside interests, extra schoolwork and part-time jobs.

You're close to your family, but your loner streak means that you're not clingy with them. As long as they understand that you need space, you should have very few arguments in the next few years.

In love Scorpion girls are warm and like to show public affection: a characteristic some of your boyfriends will hate. You'll meet lots of lively boys over the next five years, and you'll want to go out with all of them. Fine if you've split up from the last one, but you are a little prone to being unfaithful, so watch out for rows. Eventually you'll spot your true love and you will do anything to make him yours.

♐ **SAGITTARIUS**
November 23 – December 21
Flower – Hydrangea
Animal – Horse
Stone – Amethyst
Colours – Purple, autumnal colours

You're confident, creative and optimistic. People like being around you because you're honest, tolerant and into doing new things. But you do tend to think that whatever you do is right, even if your best friends disagree. This is what will cause you most arguments over the next few years. You're probably the one in class who gets involved in debates and is confident enough to put your hand up in class whether you know the answer or not. Sagittarian girls are great communicators and you're likely to find yourself working in media or teaching.

You're sociable and the best listener of all the signs. Your friends love you and they let you know it. But you will have moments of frustration. Taking on mates' problems will get you down, but within five years you'll feel less affected by it.

Love will come your way fairly easily as your confidence will help you grab the boy you want. But you won't find your love for a few years yet. Sagittarian girls need to find out about the world and themselves before they are prepared to share that with anyone else.

♑ CAPRICORN

December 22 – January 20

Flower – Fuchsia

Animal – Goat

Stone – Jet

Colours – Black, grey

You know exactly what you want and you're deter- mined to get it. You're hard-working and you learn from your mistakes. Whether it's schoolwork, part-time jobs or playing sports, you always reach your targets. You like to look good and you're very concerned with people's opinions of you.

Capricorn girls are faithful to their families, and generally you all get on quite well. But you will have a few fights over the next two years and it'll be your fault. If you've got your sights on something you want outside your family, you won't have time for them at all and you'll be totally unaware of their feelings. You are similar with your friends, but they tend to forgive you more. Also they know that you are a true friend and are never going to go off with new mates just because they might be cool.

When it comes to boys, you suddenly become very emotional. Expect fun over the next few years, but expect a broken heart too. You'll be clingy and possessive with boys that you really like, but you'll say 'I love you' when you really mean it. Amazing snogs are on the cards!

≈≈ **AQUARIUS**
January 21 – February 19
Flower – Pansy

Animal – Fox
Stone – Garnet
Colours – Bright pink, electric green

You're original, independent and full of ideas. Aquarians are real team players, which is very promising for work ahead. At the moment you find school restricts your ideas and has too many rules for you. In five years' time your eccentricity will be rewarded; till then you're going to have to argue, and more often than not, you'll lose.

You flit between loving being in a gang, and needing time alone. At home, your parents will think you're being 'teenage' when you disappear off to your room, but in three or four years they'll realise this is you, not a stage. You can be a bit tactless, so although your mates love being around you, you do upset them sometimes.

Aquarian girls are the unusual zodiac sign when it comes to love. You're scared of commitment, so you'll be spending the next few years enjoying youth, meeting boys and having fun. Within three years you still won't understand why your friends put so much emphasis on boyfriends. But when the time is right, you'll let yourself go and you will have a very deep relationship.

♓ PISCES

February 20 – March 20
Flower – Lupin
Animal – Eagle
Stone – Carnelian
Colours – Silver-blue, grey

You're considerate, dreamy and romantic. You're never in a hurry and although people think you're vague, you do get things done. You're very giving; in the future you're likely to work in a helping profession, like nursing, but you're creative too. At school you're learning to manage your time and workload; in the next few years this skill will be invaluable.

Your untidiness is going to be the key to most of your family rows, and the fact that you drift off so much into a dreamworld. But your family adores you and you're at your happiest at home.

Being so open with your mates will pay off – those friendships should stand the test of time. But you'll also meet lots of interesting people in the next five years, who will become life-long friends.

Piscean girls are very eager to please boys, and lots of boys will want to go out with you, but you'll have trouble sorting the good from the bad.

The Pisces girl is blinded by love. If a boy's not treating you well, you won't see it. But when you find a good lad, there is no other sign that will have such a perfect romance. Think of all your favourite soppy movies and double the soppiness!

Tips for all Goddesses

Learn as much as you can about yourself and take on board things other people say, even if they're hurtful. Your future will be so much easier if you really understand yourself.

Chapter 6

FUTURE FRIENDS?

I Ching

You might be bosom buddies now, but will you be arch enemies next year? It's hard even to consider that you and your mate might not be so close later on, but actually it's no bad thing. Sometimes friendships are right for a time, but aren't destined to last. You both might be far happier to be best mates with someone else. On the other hand, the mates you've got now may stay with you till you're eighty!

What is I Ching?

I Ching is an ancient Chinese way of determining change. It uses hexagrams – little line-drawn shapes – to point towards how things will alter.

How does it work?

Get three coins and a pencil to draw on the chart on the next page. If when you throw the coins on to the floor or a table, you get mostly heads, draw a straight line – a yin (only about a centimetre and a half long: ————). If you get mostly tails draw a broken line – a yang (the same length, but with a tiny gap in its middle: —— ——).

Throw the three coins another five times, to get five more lines. Draw each line on the page about 5mm above the last, running parallel to it. You'll then have a six-line diagram – or hexagram – which will tell you about change, for example:

What can it tell you about yourself?

Because I Ching is the ancient way of predicting change, it's the perfect tool for determining how your friendships will develop.

Write down a list of your six closest friends starting with your favourite mate. Throw the three coins six times for each friend, and with each throw think of a different word or moment that reminds you of them.

Name	**hexagram**
1	
2	
3	
4	
5	
6	

Now check the guide underneath for each of the six friends, to see what I Ching has to say about how your relationships will develop.

All straight lines

You two have definitely got a bond, but you're likely to get on each other's nerves from time to time. This could last but you've got to strike out and start doing something to improve relations now! Keep going till things run smoothly, but don't try too hard to make things perfect. That will feel false and unnatural. You should be able to last into the future.

All broken lines

This is tough; your future as mates is in his/her hands, and you're going to have to wait and see. Whatever you do, you can't be the one to make your friendship last or break up. But don't get upset, your relationship will start to go in the direction in which it's intended. Chill and you'll actually enjoy any changes that arise.

One straight line – the rest broken

You two are like Minnie and Mickey. You're meant to be together and there's no reason to anticipate any dramatic change in your friendship. Any rows that happen in the future should smooth themselves out with the mellow vibes between you both.

One broken line – the rest straight

If you two are just getting to know each other, this is going to blossom into a great, happy, fun relationship. But if this is an old mate, the friendship is actually going to disappear and a new companion will step in. However long you've known this person, your future plans will include a group that he or she won't be involved with.

Two straight lines – the rest broken

You've got a big argument or disagreement on the way. But this needn't end your time as mates. Sometimes friendships are better if they're not completely smooth. A huge bout of bitchiness can be just what you need to clear out any moans and groans so that you two can get on with having nothing but fun for a while.

Two broken lines – the rest straight

Competition is going to be the problem between you two. It could be healthy, where you just spur each other on, but if it starts to get more serious, you might find that that's what's going to tear you apart.

Three broken, three straight

This is a perfect time to think about your friendship. If you know it's worth saving, bring up any problems and face them now. It's a great time to be totally honest and love one another.

Best mates?

Now that you've started thinking about how your friendships could develop, it's time to ask yourself some questions about your best mate. Just because you hang out with her all the time, it doesn't mean you're right for each other.

Ask yourself these ten questions, counting up how many times you say yes in your head:

- Does your best friend have less time for you when she has a boyfriend?
- Do you worry about little arguments you have?
- Does your mum tell you that she thinks you're bad for one another?
- Do you wish you were spending more time with someone else?
- Do you keep secrets from her?

59

- Is she the sort of friend who you wouldn't take to every occasion?
- Does she confide in someone else over you?
- Do you take longer than two days to patch up rows?
- Has a teacher or friend told you that she's a bad influence on you?
- Do you get very jealous of things she has that you don't?

If you said 'yes' more than five times

You two have become close this year, but this is probably more to do with circumstance than real friendship. In the next three months you'll notice a change. Within a year you probably won't hang out at all. The trouble is you've got too many niggling problems; you're not having screaming matches but you're not incredibly happy. You'll find that when one of you really needs the other she won't be there, and that will start the change in your relationship.

Start putting emphasis on where your friendship works best. Maybe you two are great for silly pulling nights out. If that's the case start searching for the mate who's there for you when you want to have serious chats.

If you said 'no' more than five times

Your friendship might have its ups and downs but essentially you two hang out because you understand each other. You work on more than one level. You're probably as happy giggling over celeb boys that you fancy as you are moaning about family niggles. You two are likely to sit next to each other well into your A levels and could keep in touch for the rest of your lives. Start thinking about areas of the friendship you'd like to improve though. If you've got a best mate who really is your soul mate it's worth putting in the work early. It would be such a shame if a silly row and too much pride ruined a beautiful friendship.

A tip for Goddesses of Cool

You are great when it comes to friendship, so be a true friend and look out for fall-outs between your mates which you might be able to help.

Chapter 7

HOW WILL YOU COPE WITH THE PEOPLE IN YOUR HOUSE?

Birth Hours

Even if your home life is perfect, every now and then you'll be caught up in arguments that would put the worst 'EastEnders' family to shame. But don't worry. Those rows aren't just down to you, your big sister or your younger brother, they're more likely to be due to personality clashes. And let's face it, they are inevitable – you don't choose your family like you choose your mates, and it's unlikely that you won't have clashes. However what you may not have realised is that you and your siblings were probably born with these temperaments.

What are birth hours?

Birth hours are the slots of time in which you were born. They go in two-hour periods, so ask your mum for yours and your brothers' and sisters'. (If you're an only child but you want to find out why you row with your parents or cousins, the same method can be used.)

How do they work?

In the same way that horoscopes tell you about the influence of the Sun and stars on the day you were born, birth hours tell you about the influence of the Sun on the exact time you were born.

What can they tell you about yourself?

Your birth hours will tell you about the traits you were born with – the ones you can't really change. But this prediction will also tell you more about your strengths, so that you can think rationally about how to improve the way you get on with your family.

Birth hours explained

See if your family disputes fit in with the birth hour guide:

0.01 a.m. – 2 a.m.

You're a night owl, who loves showing off your eccentricities.

2.01 a.m. – 4 a.m.

You're a dreamer, who is either very happy or very sad.

4.01 a.m. – 6 a.m.

You're bright and enthusiastic, but not aware of other's feelings.

6.01 a.m. – 8 a.m.

You strive for what you want, but think of yourself first.

8.01 a.m. – 10 a.m.

You're punctual and efficient.

10.01 a.m. – 12 noon

You're lively and happy but you can be irritable.

12.01 p.m. – 2 p.m.
You're a passionate person, so you love or hate.

2.01 p.m. – 4 p.m.
You're quite chilled out and do anything to avoid arguments.

4.01 p.m. – 6 p.m.
You're a family person, so you do what you can to make others happy.

6.01 p.m. – 8 p.m.
You aren't always chirpy but everyone likes your fun nature.

8.01 p.m. – 10 p.m.
You always intrigue others but they don't often understand you.

10.01 p.m. – Midnight
You drag behind but you're wise and learn from mistakes.

Why am I like that?
Other funny little traits you have can be down to

your birth – again ask your mum if she had you early, late or roughly on the due day. Also the order in which you and your brothers and sisters were born in will affect you, i.e. being the oldest child is very different from being the youngest one.

Born late – You're selfish, careless and usually late, but you've got a chilled-out attitude that everyone loves.

Born near due day – You're fussy and have high expectations of others, but you're perceptive, accurate and caring.

Born early – You're snappy and jump into arguments too quickly, but you're enthusiastic and full of energy.

Eldest child – You can be selfish, moody and over-sensitive, but you're very responsible and loving.

Middle child – You're generally chilled out, but you are a big attention-seeker. You are the most likely sibling to burst into tears in a row.

Youngest child – You're impatient and demanding, but you're also creative and experimental.

A tip for all Goddesses

Families will fall out, so don't expect that all your problems should be cleared up in one day. There are going to be lots of times that you'll feel like your brothers and sisters must have been adopted from an alien family. Don't be too hard on them; deep down you know you love them really.

Chapter 8

WILL YOU MAKE YOUR PARENTS PROUD?

They drive us absolutely bonkers, but we still can't help wanting our parents' recognition.

'I wasn't getting on with my mum at all,' explains seventeen-year-old Amy from Worcester. 'I think it started because I was seeing someone she didn't approve of. We argued so much that even when my boyfriend and I had broken up, she still seemed to take every opportunity to put me down. Finally, I was doing the lead role in a play with my drama club and I didn't even bother asking her to come and see the performance. When the show had finished I got loads of praise, but the only person I really wanted to hear say "Well done" was my mum.

'The following day, when she heard that the show had been on, she was so upset that I cried and finally we made up. I wished I'd swallowed my pride and invited her. It was stupid to think that the one person whose approval I've needed since I was three years old wasn't there at my big moment.'

WILL YOU MAKE THEM PROUD?

Will they be patting you on the back or threatening to kick your butt? Answer the following questions and ring **a**, **b** or **c** as you go.

1 What's your favourite subject at school?
a Netball. 1
b Art. 5
c Maths. 10

2 What comment appeared most on your last school report?
a 'Is very bright, but doesn't . . .' 5

69

b '. . . tries hard, but doesn't always achieve . . .' 10

c '. . . needs to apply herself more.' 1

3 What's your mum or dad's favourite saying?

a 'You really should get a part-time job.' 10

b 'You don't ever help around the house.' 5

c 'You're lazy.' 1

4 How do you think you're doing at school?

a Better than ever. 10

b Worse than last year. 1

c Pretty much the same as last year. 5

5 How do you see your teachers in general?

a As people who you occasionally get on with. 5

b As people you can go to with problems. 10

c As people from another planet. 1

6 Have you set yourself goals for this year?

a No, it's not something you've thought of. 1

b A couple, but haven't done anything about them yet. 5

c Yes, and you've fulfilled some. 10

7 What would you most like in the next year?
a More interests. 5
b A boyfriend. 1
c To pass all your exams. 10

8 Where do you see yourself in five years' time?
a Working in a job that pays well. 5
b Furthering your education. 10
c No idea whatsoever. 1

9 How much do you tell your parents about your life?
a Very little, you'd sooner they didn't know. 1
b Discuss school, friends and interests, but not boys. 5
c Tell them everything. 10

10 How would you describe your group of mates?
a A mixture – some just want to have fun, others are more serious. 5
b Very driven. 10
c None of them are bothered about school. 1

Now add up your scores.

71 – 100

Your parents will be singing your praises to everyone including those old great-aunts you thought had died years ago. You're the sort of person who not only needs your parents' approval, you actually get it, and if you carry on this way, you'll certainly make Mum and Dad proud. Be careful not to let all your interests or schoolwork slip though; it's really tempting if a cute boy or partying social life come your way. That doesn't mean you can't have lots of fun too – it's a matter or balance. Make sure that you don't start doing things just to please your family. You have to go with what you want in life, not what other people want for you. If you're open with everyone you should have no problems and lots of praise and maybe even cash rewards in store!

35 – 70

At the moment you're doing OK, but there's room for improvement in your parents' minds. If they start being a bit hard on you that's just them hoping to spur you on. If you take notice, they're bound to be happy with how hard you work at school and how much you put into life in general. Although it seems like they do, mums and dads don't actually expect miracles, so don't wear yourself out trying to be Superchild. All they want of you is your best, but if you think they're pushing you too hard, tell them – they're not mind-readers. If you put a bit more effort into school, work and hobbies and less into boys and CDs, they'll be embarrassing you with 'My daughter's so great . . .' stories.

34 and under

At the moment you're probably bored stiff with comments like 'Why can't you be more like . . .?' Your mum and dad are letting off steam because they can see that you're not trying hard enough. But there's no reason why that can't change. Firstly, don't get upset and think you're useless. Instead, have a long think about whether you've been unlucky lately or whether you've been making an effort and just haven't been rewarded. If you know there's more you can do to please them, and more importantly, please yourself, do it. The more you achieve the better you'll feel about yourself and the more praise you'll get – and praise makes everyone feel good. Whatever happens, don't give up to spite your mum and dad if they're driving you crazy. You'll only hurt yourself.

73

HOW TO KEEP IT A HOME SWEET HOME

- Never slam doors; that gives them a reason to harp on about teenage mood swings, one of the most annoying phrases some parents use.
- Before you argue, take a deep breath and think about what you're going to say. The wrong comment might really hurt them, even if they don't let you know it.
- If you think that they're honestly in the wrong, go and calm down and list your reasons. Then, when the atmosphere is calm, explain why you think you've got a valid point.
- If you think they're being too hard on you, but you're scared to say something, have a chat with a teacher or older friend or relative. Someone else's perspective will help you see who's in the right.
- No matter how angry you all are with each other, let them know how much you care.
- Remember they are only human too. They're going to make mistakes and have bad days just like the rest of us.

Chapter 9

HAPPY FAMILIES AND FRIENDSHIPS

Numerology and Feng Shui

Every relationship goes through its rough patches. The key to happiness between you and your friends and families is understanding each other's faults and forgiving one another. The easiest way to start ironing out any little problems is to think about your personality and how you may clash against or complement the personalities of the people around you. A really good divinatory tool for that is numerology.

What is numerology?

Numerology is a very old prediction tool which uses numbers relevant to your life to tell you what's going to happen.

How does it work?

Numerology can use all different numbers taken from aspects of your life, but to find out what personalities are like – which will help you have happier relationships – the best number is the birth number. To work out what your birth number is, write out your full date of birth on a piece of paper. For example, if you were born on 5 June 1985, write out 5 6 1985. Now add all those numbers together, and keep adding the totals till you get only one figure. For example, 5+6+1+9+8+5=34 then add 3+4=7. Your birth number would be seven.

What can it tell you about yourself?

Your birth number tells you about character traits that were determined on the day you were born. They're the characteristics that you might be able to control, but you can't change – if you're stubborn, at some point everyone's going to know about it!

How well are your relationships adding up?
To find out how your home relationships and friendships could be happier, work out your birth number and two family members' numbers. We've suggested a parent and a sibling but it could be other people in the family – it might be good to choose someone you're having troubles with. Then work out birth numbers for three friends.

Your birth number

Parent

Sibling

Friend

Friend

Friend

What your birth numbers mean

1 Number 1 people are leaders.

Good traits: Strong, creative, independent.

Bad traits: Bossy, selfish, dominant.

2 Number 2 people are deep in thought.

Good traits: Gentle, charming, perceptive.

Bad traits: Over-sensitive, lacking confidence.

3 Number 3 people are full of energy.

Good traits: Independent, hard-working, talented.

Bad traits: Talk too much, very critical.

4 Number 4 people are practical.

Good traits: Endure anything, not materialistic.

Bad traits: Rebellious, isolated.

5 Number 5 people are impulsive.

Good traits: Bubbly, quick-thinking, successful.

Bad traits: Strung out, quick-tempered.

6 Number 6 people are trustworthy.

Good traits: Balanced, romantic, reliable.

Bad traits: Stubborn, fearful of arguments.

7 Number 7 people are spiritual.

Good traits: Lucky, capable of influencing, almost psychic.

Bad traits: Introverted, unpractical.

8 Number 8 people are individuals.

Good traits: Strong willpower, deep, successful.

Bad traits: Seem cold, bad communicators, sad.

9 Number 9 people are outgoing.

Good traits: Brave, determined, will go out and do it.

Bad traits: Clumsy, argumentative.

HAPPIER FAMILIES AND FRIENDS

Number 1 people get on best with number 2 people. To improve relationships with the other numbers, you've got to give up your desire to be in control. Before you bark an order, let someone else have a go, and remember your way isn't the only way.

Number 2 people get on best with number 1 people, because you prefer a submissive role. To get on with the other numbers you have to earn their respect. Try being a bit louder and think about what you want, instead of always making do with what you are given.

Number 3 people get on best with other 3s and number 6 and number 9 people. The other numbers find it a bit hard to keep up with your energy. Slow down, calm down, and make them see that you're not a flighty girl, that you do have substance and that you can be relaxed.

Number 4 people really gel with numbers 1, 2, 7 and 8: they see you as steady and easy, but other people don't understand your rebellious side. Make an effort to be social and behave like them – it'll feel weird at first, but eventually you'll be accepted for who you are.

Number 5 people are really close to other number 5s, but you're also the lucky birth number who gets on with everyone. The only trait that people really don't understand about you is why you let things get to you so much. Concentrate on relaxing – once you're more chilled everyone will love you.

Number 6 people are great at making friends with all the birth numbers, but getting along with family who are other numbers is a bit harder. Don't be set in your ways with them, and don't make such a big deal out of family tiffs. They're going to happen and they're not the end of the world.

Number 7 people intrigue all numbers but are not really understood by number 1 or number 3 people. To bond with them, offer to do things they're into for a change. Your interests are harder to share for those birth numbers so take the initiative yourself.

Number 8 people get on best with number 4 and number 8 people. The others misunderstand you. Do something nice for them – make them see that you're not cold and uncaring, and try to be more open about how you feel. Your intensity might be scaring them, but it could also be interesting them.

Number 9 people are special, because when you multiply your number by any other number you add up to 9 still (2x9=18, 1+8=9). That might be the reason that the other numbers treat you with awe. If you do something wrong you're likely to be forgiven. And strangely that's where the trouble starts. Number 9 people are seen as favourites, so try to be super nice to anyone prone to jealousy.

FENG SHUI

To improve your family relationships and friendships, spend some time alone in your bedroom! Why not try a little Feng Shui?

What is Feng Shui?

Feng Shui is the Eastern art of balancing and improving the flow of natural energies in our surroundings to make life much happier for us.

How does it work?

Feng Shui makes you look around yourself (in this chapter at your bedroom) and think, Is that vase of flowers going to be positive there, or would it be better somewhere else? It suggests where to place – or not place – things in your room to help energies flow more peacefully.

What can it tell you about yourself?

Feng Shui doesn't exactly give us more information about ourselves but it can give pointers on how we can feel better, have better relationships, or improve our lives.

YOUR BEDROOM

You go to sleep there at night, it's the first place you see when you wake up. It's your haven when everyone's driving you mad, and it's the place that you spend most of your life. It's not surprising then that your bedroom can have such a huge effect on your life and your relationships.

Different spots in your bedroom represent different areas of your life. So there are changes you can make to these areas to make things happier.

1 Wealth	2 Fame	3 Love
4 Family	5 Unity	6 Creativity
7 Self- improvement	8 Career	9 Friends

◄ base-line

Now stand in the doorway of your bedroom looking in with the grid in front of you. The base-line of the grid is where your bedroom door is, so that as you look at your room, your Wealth corner (1) should be the furthest left-hand corner from you. In your head, split the room up into nine.

You can try to improve lots of areas of your life using this basic Feng Shui plan, but for now it's best to concentrate on your mates and your family – if those relationships are going smoothly, other stuff sort of falls into place. So concentrate on getting areas 4, 5 and 9 – Family, Unity and Friends – sorted.

FAMILY AREA

In your Family area you want to create as much of a calm atmosphere as possible – let's face it, your biggest rows are with the people you live with.

How to Feng Shui Family (area 4)

Put in a water feature to make life flow calmly. If you can get a small running water ornament – Oriental style, from gift shops or hippy-style stores – that's ideal. Next best thing is getting goldfish, even one of those pretend tanks. But if that's not possible get a small picture or photo of a river, lake or sea to hang on the wall or put on a surface. Then, whenever you have a row with your little brother or your mum, pour a little water into a saucer and put it in the area overnight as well.

UNITY AREA

In your Unity area you want to create a bonding feeling. With both your family and friends, making sure you understand each other is really important.

How to Feng Shui Unity (area 5)

This is kind of a difficult spot because you may have a bed in that space, or it may be the clear part of your room. If you can, put a friendship bracelet there, or tie two pieces of ribbon together. If there's no obvious place to put them, slip them under a rug, or your bed, or suspend them from the ceiling. If you feel like you are growing apart from someone though, place it under your pillow for a few nights.

FRIENDS AREA

In your Friends area you want to create a feeling of happiness and luck. Sometimes friendships go through bad times for really silly reasons, and you want to avoid that.

How to Feng Shui Friends (area 9)

Put something red in that spot: it's the colour that brings best fortune. You can use anything you like – red silk flowers, red beads, a red picture even a red T-shirt. Also put in photos of you and your mates having brilliant times. Try to have a good mixture, not just ten shots of one mate: no matter how close you are, everyone needs more than one friend. If you've got a pin-board with pictures of your mates, put that up in the friendship area too. But if you've got old photos of someone you've since fallen out with, who you don't intend to see

again, take them down. Bad friendship memories
will influence your good ones.

You can keep an eye on the other areas of your
room and your life by following these tips:

Wealth area (1)

This is the part of your room concerned with
money and material stuff. It's a good idea to put a
valued, expensive item here, like a stereo – it
means you appreciate how fortunate you are.
Always keep the valued item clean.

Fame/reputation area (2)

Put something here to signify your goal. If you really
want to be a champion swimmer, put up a photo
of you at a swimming gala. Also keep something
there (it can be hidden) of where you'd like to get
to. If you want to be a writer, keep your favourite
book there. This area will then be a reminder of
what you want now and where you want to be.

Love area (3)

If you're in love you might want to keep a picture of
the boy, but unless you're really sure of him it is

better to keep this area more general. Concentrate on thinking about you in your love life. Keep flowers here to make your love life feel alive, bright and happy. Don't keep anything in this area that reminds you of a bad romance. Negative breeds negative.

Project area (6)
This is concerned with your interests. Whether you're really into a sport, or dancing, mechanics or music, this area, if kept properly, will help you keep focused on your hobby. Give it a work-type feel, maybe get some in-trays or drawers here, and always keep it tidy and organised. Keep any important documents to do with your hobby here too.

Knowledge area (7)
This area is about everything you are learning in your life. It's a good area to keep clear for you and your thoughts. If possible, spend a little time every day or two, just quietly sitting in this area. Give yourself a few moments where you can shut your eyes and let your thoughts waft through your mind.

Your life ahead area (8)
This part of the room is probably near your door,

and is the area that is actually opening up to your new life. It is concerned with the future, the rest of your education and your career. Don't keep your childhood items here, so if you've still got toys or possessions from your earlier life, keep them in another part of your room. Instead keep something you think is lucky here, maybe just stuck to the back of your door. If you don't have a possession like that just stick up a picture that you like.

GENERAL FRIEND AND FAMILY FENG SHUI

- Don't have anything visible that reminds you of bad times.
- Keep your Family, Unity and Friends areas clean and clutter free.
- As your relationships develop and change – for example, your older brother might go away to college, or you might become close friends with someone new – move things around in their areas and add new items.

A tip for all Goddesses
Try not to go to sleep at night without fixing an argument with a brother, sister, parent or friend, otherwise you'll wake to another bad day.

Chapter 10

IN FOR A SPELL OF POPULARITY?

Letters of Fortune

How do you fit in with your gang? Are you going to be a leader or a follower? Are you a good listener or do you alienate mates? Are you going to be popular or not? The letters of fortune can help you learn about the way you interact with your friends.

What are the letters of fortune?

The letters of fortune are the letters in your name. The most prominent letter is the first one of your first name, but each is significant.

How do the letters of fortune work?

Get a pen and paper and jot down the letters of your first name. Use the name you're most commonly called by. If Catherine is the name on your birth certificate, but everybody calls you Cathy, use Cathy. Then find each letter in the list underneath. For the first letter of your name take on board everything that the letters of fortune say, for example for Cathy, C is the most important and accurate letter to describe you. Then jot down what all the other letters say about you too.

What can they tell you about yourself?

You'll be left with lots of descriptions of your personality and how you interact with your friends. If similar traits appear often, take notice. If you think the description is inaccurate ask a friend for a second opinion. Finally, the great thing about letters of fortune is that they allow you to be flexible. If Cathy would be more positive with a K, you can adjust the spelling of your name. You don't have to change your register or anything, but you could be known as Kathy in your gang. You can also drop or add letters to make yourself a more positive member of your group, e.g. Ally can change to Ali, if that helps.

LETTERS OF FORTUNE

A Your enthusiasm can inspire your mates. You're likely to travel far away, so you may leave some friendships. You can achieve through hard work and your skill.

B You're prone to upsetting friends because you're so honest, and you should start thinking before you act. But you work out problems really well.

C You understand your mates brilliantly and you're clever, so people look up to you. But if there are little niggling things, you can't be bothered to sort them out.

D You're very wise at sorting out arguments, but you can be a bit direct, so your mates might be put off taking your advice. You won't be scared though – taking risks may mean you have the best relationships.

E You're calm and always see both sides, and because you're versatile your mates respect you and should continue to do so. You're not quite sure what your friends think of you: don't assume it's bad and it won't be.

F You're good at making friendships last and you're very good at working as part of a gang.

91

You've got an exciting future so you may be taken away from your mates, but when you return they'll still love you.

G You like your own space but you connect with friends who've got similar interests. You're practical so you tend to get through problems. You'll be very popular in a small circle.

H You're not very good at coping with comments that are close to home. You've got loads of talents that your friends admire but if you go on about them, you'll alienate your closest mates.

I You're warm and if you offer your friends an ear when they need one, you'll be seen as an important member of the gang. You're good at noticing your friends' positives.

J You've got the power to help others; use your energy that way and you'll be happy. You have the ability to sense good and bad; rely on it.

K If one of the gang needs to confide in you they know you can keep a secret. Your independent soul means that you like being alone.

L You're seen as the spiritual one; use your powers. You're prone to being envious, so try not to let it get in the way of closeness.

M You need to feel comfortable. Don't be tempted

to play with emotions, you'll regret it.

N You worry about situations that haven't yet occurred. Don't make snap decisions when it comes to the people closest to you.

O Keep being honest, friends appreciate it. Loyalty and love will keep you close in your group.

P You can be down-to-earth and wise, but you must make sure that you use these talents. If you act all superior your closest friends will feel insecure.

Q You love seeing people in the best light, but don't expect too much from people. Be logical about what arises.

R You like to be a bit creative and wild, and that's why you're loved. You've got the ability to get friends to go along with what you want but don't persuade them to act selfishly.

S You're great at getting things done, not just for yourself, but for your closest friends too. Your greatest gift is that you make people happy.

T You will always be on the look-out for close relationships but you can't sit still for long. You're the spontaneous one.

U Temptation to be too demanding should be avoided, but you're a perfectionist so you try to make everything, even friendship, just right.

V You don't always agree with the rest of the gang. When it comes to hanging out, you often can't be bothered. But you're practical, so remember that we all need people.

W You're a great shoulder to cry on, and one of the most dependable girls in the group, but don't go along with foolish plans at the drop of a hat.

X You love nothing more than being out with your friends. You're the life and soul, but can also be a bit of a dreamer. Stay grounded or you might come across as flaky.

Y Take your friends' advice more often, otherwise you'll find yourself getting into trouble. You've always got the strength to stand up for what you believe in and it's noticed.

Z You're good at figuring out what's going on within the group, but you're also a bit vain. Be careful not to think too much of yourself; people won't always admire you as much as you admire yourself.

From the description that the letters of fortune supplied, you should now have a better idea of what to do or not to do to make friendships smoother. Get your friends to do the same and work out how well you should interact.

WILL YOU BE MISS POPULAR?

Are you going to be the queen of the gang this year? Look at what's going on now to find out. Read the questions and ring Y for yes or N for no.

Do you:

1 always get phoned first with gossip?   Y N

2 leave one of your mates out of social stuff? Y N

3 have a different best mate from a year ago? Y N

4 bitch with a mate about another when
     she's not around?   Y N

5 get invited to lots of parties?   Y N

6 feel confident to approach boys?   Y N

7 think your friends say they'd like to be
     more like you?   Y N

8 get excited about getting to school in the
     morning?   Y N

9 care what people think of you?   Y N

10 like being the centre of attention?   Y N

95

Now count up how many Ys and Ns you collected.

7 or more Ys

Hello, Miss Popular! You really are a hit with your mates and if you fell out with them, you wouldn't be lonely for long, because there will always be someone else who wants to hang out with you. But be careful. This is fine as a temporary state, but putting too much importance on popularity means that you might overlook the really important stuff, like having a seriously close friend who'll be there no matter what. People need to know that you care about them, and that you're not just using them to make yourself look better. No matter how much they want to give you their friendship, if you're not giving something back, they won't stick around for ever.

4 – 6 Ys

You're a good dependable mate. You've got a small gang who love you and if you carry on as you are, there's no reason for that to change. The future should see you meeting lots of new friends but also managing to keep old mates close. Don't be tempted to go for higher status in your group.

You like the idea of being the loudest, sassiest girl in class, but it's not you. Friends will see through pretending to be what you're not, and they won't be impressed.

3 or less Ys

You're too caring as a mate. You do everything your friends tell you to, because you don't feel confident enough to stand up to them. You've got a sweet nature that people who've known you for years will appreciate, but newer friends might abuse this. Don't be a doormat – stand up for yourself and let them know that you want to be included and treated equally. If they won't do that for you you're in the wrong gang. If you feel like you're treated as the butt of the class jokes, get yourself more interests outside school.

Are you being bullied by your mates?

You might be excusing your friends because you don't to lose them, but if they do any of these five things then deep down they are damaging you:

- Call you names that make you unhappy even though you laugh along.

97

- Persuade you to go along with things you don't want to.
- Play tricks on you that make you sad when you're alone.
- Spread rumours about you that aren't true.
- Put you down in front of others.

If you feel like you're being bullied you can call the Anti-Bullying Campaign for advice or support on 020 7378 1446.

A tip for Goddesses of Calm

Going for a quiet life and putting up with your lot is not going to make you happy. Make some noise!

Chapter 11

ARE YOU THE GODDESS OF LOVE?

Cartomancy

When it comes to boys, love and all the soppy stuff, some of us are born experts and some of us just don't get it! If you're in the second group, you spend your time baffled as to how your best mate has just managed to find yet another boy to follow her around like a love-sick puppy. But we all have strengths when it comes to love, it's just that we aren't all great flirts or great communicators.

Fate has some love treats in store for every girl. Is love going to be a smooth ride for you? Have you found him already? If you have, is he really right for you? To try and find out more, have a game of cards.

What is cartomancy?

Cartomancy is a prediction tool using normal playing cards, but it originates from Tarot.

How does it work?

You start with your Goddess card, the queen of hearts when you're trying to predict love. Around that, you deal out seven groups of three cards. Each card has a different meaning, and if one card lies next to another, that can alter their meanings. Like Tarot, the cards are there for your interpretation. For example, the Death card in Tarot isn't usually sinister, it's just probably referring to something that's coming to an end, like your school year, or a friendship.

What can it tell you about yourself?

Cartomancy makes you have a good look at what's going on around you and it can hint at what's going to be going on in your love life in the future.

ARE YOU THE GODDESS OF LOVE?

Is there lots of romance on the cards? Deal them and see.

What to do

First get yourself a normal pack of cards and take out the jokers. Then find the queen of hearts and lie it on the floor, face up with quite a bit of space around it. Next, shuffle the pack then place three cards face down next to each other on the left hand side of the queen. Making a semicircle around the queen lay out six more groups, so that the last group of three – the seventh group – is to the right hand side of the queen.

Then think of a love subject – it can be anything from Who do I really fancy? to Is this boy bad for me? Turn over the three cards and look through the guide to their meanings below. All the card meanings are open to interpretation so think hard about what they could mean to your life. For example if you are told to watch out for a boy with light hair, it might not be about a potential boyfriend, it might be a warning about a boy who's getting in the way of you and another boy's potential romance. Also if you get a card combination (see page 105) it cancels out single card meanings.

Once you've done the first group, go around the semicircle giving yourself a different topic for each group of three.

♥ HEARTS

Ace Big love and really happy.

King Look out for a boy with light-coloured hair.

Jack A really good mate.

Ten You'll get some of what you want.

Nine Wish card – you can make him happen.

Eight You'll get asked to a party.

Seven Watch out, he might be unreliable.

Six Out of the blue, something good will happen.

Five You'll be jealous.

Four He'll put you off till later.

Three Be careful.

Two You'll succeed.

♦ DIAMONDS

Ace A love letter is on its way.

King Watch out for a stubborn boy.

Queen A flirty blonde girl.

Jack A family member might let you down.

Ten You're off somewhere new.

Nine You won't be able to sit still.

Eight A long-term boyfriend is a long time off.

Seven You're going to lose someone.

Six Listen if someone warns you off him.

Five Good news.

Four Expect some changes.

Three A row at home.

Two Wow! A big heavy relationship's on its way.

♣ CLUBS

Ace Money and love.

King A dark-haired boy will be honest with you.

Queen Be aware of a dark-haired, strong girl.

Jack A friend who's there for you.

Ten Some good luck.

Nine A mate's being stuck in their ways.

Eight You'll be upset.

Seven Could be good, but another boy might get
in the way.

103

Six You'll be glowing because school's going well.

Five A new friend.

Four Good luck could turn to bad.

Three Might be more than one love in your life.

Two Someone is against you.

♠ SPADES

Ace Your relationship will go wrong.

King A boy who wants to get to the top.

Queen Watch out for a dark girl with no morals.

Jack Your mate is too lazy to help.

Ten You'll be panicking.

Nine Bad luck's on its way.

Eight Trouble ahead.

Seven If you break up you won't be able to be just friends.

Six It's going to get better.

Five Problems, but things'll work out.

Four Jealousy is in the air.

Three A break-up is coming.

Two He'll lie to you.

CARD COMBOS

If certain cards land right next to each other, they have special meanings:

Ace of hearts and any other heart You're friends.

Ace of hearts with a heart each side of it A steamy romance!

Ace of hearts with spades either side Arguments ahead.

Ace of spades with ten of spades Something serious will happen.

Ten of hearts Cancel any bad luck cards next to it. The good luck ones are even better though.

Nine of hearts next to any bad cards Things will be in your way.

Eight of spades with nine of clubs You'll be happy.

Eight of hearts with five of hearts A gift of jewellery.

Eight of spades on the right of your Goddess card Stop the plans you're making.

Two of diamonds with two of clubs A secret message.

Now count up the number of cards in each suit you dealt in your 21 cards.

Mostly hearts

As a Goddess of love, you're very lucky! Hearts point out all the soppy stuff and emotions, so if they're turning up regularly, it might be that it's the right time for your love life. Take all the hints into consideration and think about what they could be pointing to and don't be tempted to just relate them to a boy that you fancy or are seeing. Be very honest with yourself and think about whether there is someone else who'd be better suited to you. If your heart cards are saying something very positive, but you're not quite sure what they mean, ask your best mate. Sometimes our friends are more aware of what's going on in our love lives than we are!

Mostly diamonds

Diamond cards concern themselves with all the stuff that happens in your life outside of you, or your mates, boyfriends and home life. Basically, they're hinting at things like school or outside interests. If you're turning over lots of diamonds, maybe the cards are suggesting that you aren't a Goddess of Love at the moment, because you've got more important things to do. Whenever you enter a new relationship, or want to start flirting, it's great to have your own independent strengths – they make you more interesting to boys anyway. When you've achieved things for you on your own, you can start thinking about achieving something for you with someone else.

Mostly clubs

Clubs point out all the success you're going to have in the future, so it might be that your best time as a Goddess of Love is yet to come. If you find that you've got an equal mixture of mostly clubs and mostly hearts though, it's possible that you've got lots of powers of love now, and that something you're beginning will last well into the future. It may be that love isn't going to be where your success lies over the next few years, so think about the meanings carefully – they may be suggesting that you'll be a county tennis player before you find a boyfriend.

Mostly spades

You might have potential as the Goddess of Love, but you've got a lot to watch out for. Spades are the cards that point out what dangers are ahead for you, so if you're turning over lots of them, especially with lots of hearts, you're in for a romantic but very bumpy ride. It might be that the cards are trying to tell you what you already know – that you're going for someone who just isn't right for you. So think carefully before you jump into anything. You need to be sure you're doing it for the right reasons. If you find that you're turning over mostly spades and diamonds or clubs, maybe you should be paying more attention to interests outside of boys.

A tip for all Goddesses

If you feel that you're getting equal amounts of suits, go with your instincts. All divinatory tools are only that – tools. Your future's in your hands, and sometimes you just need to look hard in the mirror and ask yourself what's going on in your life.

Chapter 12

WILL YOU PULL YOUR DREAM BOY?

Palmistry

The thing to remember about love is that it's spontaneous and you can't predict any certainties. You might be all set for a snogging session with Ben from down the road, only to bump into Kelvin in the chip shop and fall head over heels in love.

Want some clues about your dream boy destiny? You hold all the answers in the palm of your hand.

What is palmistry?

Palmistry is when you examine all the strange lines on your palm to find out a bit more about yourself.

How does it work?

Your right hand indicates your characteristics and your left shows the changes that will happen throughout your life. Work out which lines are which, then look at the following guide to see what your sort of lines mean. Then you'll have an idea of your own character and of what's been happening and is going to happen to you in the future.

What can it tell you about yourself?

Your right hand will give you the home truths and your left will indicate what your destiny might be. It's up to you to interpret your palms yourself, though. Think about what you can achieve by using the strengths of both hands.

READING YOUR PALM
How to start

To read your hand you can simply study it, slightly cupped, facing upwards or, for a longer look, take a photocopy.

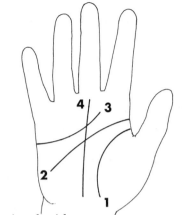

1 Your lifeline.

2 Your headline.

3 Your heartline.

4 Your line of fate.

1 The lifeline

This tells you about your lust for life.

- If it's doubled (i.e. it looks almost like two lines together, not one), you're very energetic and will be actively seeking a snog any time now.

- If your lifeline is disjointed, you're creative and will take longer to attract a boy, but it will be in a mysterious way.

- If you have little lines crossing your lifeline, there are going to be things or people getting in the way in your love life. Keep your eyes open.

2 The headline

This line is deep and stands out. If it's very long, you're bright, strong and lively.

- If your headline goes right across your palm with few curves (i.e. less than four), you're down-to-earth and can get on well with lads.

- If it's running towards the centre of your wrist, you're prone to being unrealistic.
- If it's broken, you're on track for some sad love.
- If it splits into a fork at the end, you might start dividing your time between two boys.
- If it starts near the lifeline, you're very independent, and don't need boys to be happy.

3 The heartline

If your heartline is straight, you're reserved with boys.

- If it's very deep and long (i.e. across most of your hand), you're possessive.
- If it's slightly patterned, you're a great flirt.
- If it's got lots of lines coming off it, upward ones mean a boy is on the way, downward ones mean a dry spell for a time.
- If your line is long and curved, you're very sensual. Boys love that!

4 The line of fate

If your line of fate is very strong and clear, your future is down to fate rather than your own will.

- If the line is straight and unbroken, you can expect good times, with few hiccups.

- If it starts from the headline or heartline, your triumphs will come, but not until you're older.
- If it's curved, finding your boy's not going to be easy, but you'll get there.
- If you can't seem to find a line at all, it signifies that although you'll get what you want and you'll be happy, you're probably not going to have one 'thunder and lightening' type of romance. Don't worry though, those relationships tend to bring a lot of hurt with them.

COMPATIBLE HANDS

It's not just your palms that can help you with your love life. Your hand shape says loads too, like whether you two are suited!

If you're out with a boy you like, sneak a look at his hands – far easier if he's grasping one of yours. Generally someone with a similar hand shape to you will be most compatible.

Square hands

You're practical, down-to-earth and open. You'll get on with other square and also spatulate-handed lads.

113

Spatulate hands

You're sporty and love the out-door life. You get on with other spatulate and square-handed people but would get bored with an elegant-handed boy.

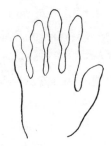

Pointy hands

You're the sort of person who copes with most situations and works hard to mentally fit in. You get on with other pointy and some elegant-handed boys.

Elegant hands

You're very emotional and take comments to heart very easily, but you're very warm. You get on with elegant and pointy hands, but square-handed boys will upset you.

A tip for Goddesses of Wild

Be prepared to have a long, good look at yourself. Otherwise when people tell you home truths you'll be shocked and hurt.

114

Chapter 13

WHO'S YOUR SOUL MATE?

Playing with Dice

Soul mates are very different from boyfriends. You can have a boyfriend for a few weeks purely because he's got a cute haircut or he's really good at tai chi, but a soul mate is somebody who is so right for you, on so many levels, that once you've found him you don't want to let him go.

Gemma was fifteen when she met hers, even though she didn't realise at first.

'I met Luke through my cousin and on our first evening together I thought he was really arrogant. I found myself arguing with him over issues that he thought he knew more about. For the next three weeks I kept telling my cousin what an idiot I thought his mate Luke was. Eventually, when I hadn't seen Luke for a month and was still talking about him, my cousin turned to me and said. "So do you want me to set up a date? I think he likes you too."

'I was in shock until he pointed out that no one had ever made such an impact on me and that the only reason I found Luke arrogant was because he had his own opinions whereas I was apparently used to people bowing down to mine. I begrudgingly agreed, although I was very excited really. When I met Luke my face broke into a huge smile. We had an amazing night where we just sat for ages in a coffee shop, talking and talking. We've been together for a year now, and although he drives me mad, I can't imagine anyone ever making me feel like he does.'

So start thinking about your soul mate, the answers could make you dotty!

What is dice prediction?
Dice prediction is when you ask dice questions about your future, the numbers you're given back suggest an answer.

How does it work?

You can do dice prediction anywhere, but if you're outside you can draw a circle with chalk to throw the dice into. If you're inside draw a circle about the size of a plate on paper. You throw the dice into the circle, and if one lands outside, throw both again. If both land outside more than once, postpone your prediction for another day. When the dice land, add up the two numbers.

Before you throw think carefully about what you want to ask the dice. Be very specific, and ask at least five questions that could help you find out if he's right for you. Ask questions like, Will we have enough to talk about? or, Has he noticed me? But don't ask the dice outright if he's your soul mate. Be more subtle and you'll learn more.

What can it tell you about yourself?

Putting some thought into your questioning might help to tell you if the boy you're thinking about is really a soul mate, or just a boyfriend.

Dice scores

2 No.

3 Be cautious.

117

4 Be sensible.

5 Good luck.

6 Definitely.

7 Keep believing.

8 Be patient.

9 Yes.

10 It's unlikely.

11 Don't be ridiculous.

12 There's a chance.

Then ask the dice if the boy you've got in mind is the right boy. If it's anything but *Yes* or *Definitely*, throw the dice again once, this time, asking Who is my soulmate?

Dice scores

1 & 1 The boy with the long features.

1 & 2 The mysterious one.

1 & 3 Not the boy with short hair.

1 & 4 The boy who you think of first each day.

1 & 5 The boy who looks embarrassed.

1 & 6 The one who has a physical feature that you don't like.

2 & 2 The clever boy.

2 & 3 The tall boy.

2 & 4 The lad who's not vain.

2 & 5 The boy with the full lips.

2 & 6 The one who gives.

3 & 3 The one who's down-to-earth.

3 & 4 The boy who thinks the same as you.

3 & 5 The mummy's boy.

3 & 6 The boy who tells you he fancies you.

4 & 4 The big flirt.

4 & 5 The lad who you think is a bit of a fool.

4 & 6 The boy who's a bit chubby.

5 & 5 The class clown.

5 & 6 The boy who your mates say isn't cute.

6 & 6 The lad that you bumped into recently.

A tip for Goddesses of Calm

Don't turn away a boy just because you know he's not your soul mate. Goddesses of Calm tend to be deeply romantic but you must realise that short flings with people who are very wrong for you are good learning experiences, and they're fun.

Chapter 14

WHO'S YOUR STAR BOY?

Astrology

He might be the sexiest boy you've ever come across, but if your love isn't written in the stars, you shouldn't even go there!

Look up the star sign of the boy you fancy on the astrological compatibility chart overleaf to see if he's your true love or your worst nightmare. This astrology chart is based on how you two will really get on. It takes into consideration long-term relationship development.

Key:

♥ Made for each other!

You might not have even noticed him before, but if you give him time you'll come to realise that you two really click. It may be that this relationship is destined to remain platonic – your two signs are so suited that you could have an amazing friendship, but look out, there's lots of love potential here too!

〰 Ups and downs!

This relationship isn't going to be easy, you'll have to take the rough with the smooth. Your problems might be as small as hating each other's taste in trainers. If that's the case you could get over it and get on with a romance. Alternatively the two of you might just have to agree to disagree and call it a day. But don't worry, there are many more signs to choose from.

✗ Don't even go there!

This boy might be an Adonis to look at, but when you get past that, you'll have nothing in common with him. Your signs just don't hit it off and at some point you'll have a massive falling out, but that's only if you don't bore each other to death first!

	Aries	Taurus	Gemini	Cancer	Leo	Virgo	Libra	Scorpio	Sagittarius	Capricorn	Aquarius	Pisces
Aries	♥	♥	♥	〰	♥	✗	〰 ▓	✗	♥	〰	♥	♥
Taurus	♥	♥	♥	♥	〰	♥	✗	〰 ▓	✗	♥	〰	♥
Gemini	♥	♥	♥	♥	♥	〰	♥	✗	〰 ▓	✗	♥	〰
Cancer	〰	♥	♥	♥	♥	♥	〰	♥	✗	〰 ▓	✗	♥
Leo	♥	〰	♥	♥	♥	♥	♥	〰	♥	✗	〰 ▓	✗
Virgo	✗	♥	〰	♥	♥	♥	♥	♥	〰	♥	✗	〰 ▓
Libra	〰 ▓	✗	♥	〰	♥	♥	♥	♥	♥	〰	♥	✗
Scorpio	✗	〰 ▓	✗	♥	〰	♥	♥	♥	♥	♥	〰	♥
Sagittarius	♥	✗	〰 ▓	✗	♥	〰	♥	♥	♥	♥	♥	〰
Capricorn	〰	♥	✗	〰	✗	♥	〰	♥	♥	♥	♥	♥
Aquarius	♥	〰	♥	✗	〰 ▓	✗	♥	〰	♥	♥	♥	♥
Pisces	♥	♥	〰	♥	✗	〰 ▓	✗	♥	〰	♥	♥	♥

Key

♥	Made for each other!
〰	Ups and downs
✗	Don't even go there!
▓	Star boy!

■ Star boy!

No matter how hard things get between you, remember that your signs are made for each other. You might have huge rows, but with this boy you'll find that you also have amazing making-up kisses. Anything that's worth having is hard work. True love is no different. He's your star boy, so do your best to make him yours!

A tip for all Goddesses

Remember, if he's not your star boy he might still be fine for a snog. Often the boys we really fancy physically are wrong for us emotionally. Have one amazing kiss for fun and leave it at that!

123

Chapter 15

WHERE LOVE LIES

Dream Analysis

What's the very last place you thought of looking for him? Well, that's probably where your perfect boy is. The after-school activity you had no intention of joining. The clapped-out sports centre you can't stand. He might even be sitting next to you. No really, some of the greatest love stories have been between two old mates who hadn't realised they were more than just good friends. To find out where Mr Right is, the best you can do is have a sleep. Sounds ridiculous, but our dreams actually say a lot more about what we want than our conscious awake self.

What is dream analysis?

Dream analysis is when you find out the meaning of the things you remember from your dreams.

How does it work?

Everything you dream about has one or more meaning. They often translate as the complete opposite of what they seem to be telling you, or they can be a vague indication of what you're really looking for in life.

What does it say about me?

Dream analysis says loads about you. Not only can it predict what might happen, it examines what's going on in your subconscious and makes you think about things in a different way. For example, you might think that you love sporty boys, but in your subconscious you might be more inspired by musicians.

Where does your love lie?

Can you find the boy of your dreams in your dreams? This quiz should not only help you find what you are looking for, but also show you where he is.

The quiz has two stages: the first is analysis about how the way you dream says something about you. Answer the questions and collect **a**s, **b**s or **c**s.

STAGE 1

1 How would you describe your dreams?

a Vague.

b Memorable.

c Very significant.

2 Which of these reminds you of a dream you had as a child?

a Being chased.

b A house.

c Playing outside.

3 What do you see most often in your dreams?

a Somewhere you don't recognise.

b Home.

c School.

4 When do memories of your dreams come to you?

a At odd times throughout the day.

b As soon as you wake up.

c When something happens to trigger the memory.

5 How honest do you think you are with yourself?

a 'I'm not, I try to behave how I think I should.'

b 'Very honest, I know myself well.'

c 'I probably kid myself sometimes.'

Now add up your **a**s, **b**s and **c**s.

Mostly 'a's

Your dreams are vague and your subconscious isn't trying to shout out any particular messages. To find out where love lies you are best to depend on your conscious self than use hints from your dreams.

Mostly 'b's

Your dreams are telling you to use everything you know well to find your boy. Your home and family are very important to you and the boy of your dreams is probably someone you know very well.

Mostly 'c's

Your dreams seem to be telling you to go out and find your adventures. You might think that you're a real home-lover but your subconscious is telling you to go far and wide. Your boy might be out there too.

STAGE 2

Now look at the three lists below. Ring all the words that you think you're dreaming about at the moment. If a certain word seems to leap out at you, ring that too. It's likely to be a dream you've forgotten.

Group 1

Fire, an instrument, friends, a party, busy places, noise, a club, lights, a song, an image change, a glass, a scuffle, being told off.

Group 2

A wide space, grass, a game, a strong boy, a flower or leaf, running, getting somewhere without knowing how, people cheering, trees and bushes.

Group 3

The sea, a letter, two people, words, a picture, a cloud, a long journey, a sunset or sunrise, quiet, someone who is indistinguishable, a ring.

Now work out which of the groups you ringed the most.

Mostly group 1

The boy of your dreams is likely to be a musician, a DJ or a party head. Deep down you like the slightly wild boy who loves going out and showing off. Spend a little more time going to new parties, record shops and busy cafés – you might just bump into him.

Mostly group 2

The boy of your dreams is likely to be the outdoors type or a footie or rugby player. You might think you need to spend all your time indoors chatting, but actually part of you yearns to be running outdoors, especially with someone you fancy. Take a few more walks in the park or maybe get involved in some outdoor pursuits.

Mostly group 3

The boy of your dreams is likely to be a poet, writer or dreamer. You might consider yourself a down-to-earth girl, but you love getting lost in romance and your daydreams. You long to travel and your inspiration comes from films and books. You'd like your travelling partner to feel the same. Take a look in the library, cafés, or at any arty film night.

THE TRUE MEANING OF COMMON LOVE DREAMS

- You kissing the boy you're going out with – True love!
- Him kissing someone else – Maybe you want a break.
- A male stranger – Someone you fancy has a side to their personality they're hiding.
- A ring – You want commitment. That could be love, or it could be that you want a friend to commit to a long-term project with you.
- A hand outstretched – You want friendship, not love.

Tip for all Goddesses

If you enjoy looking into dream analysis, leave a pen and pad by your bed. As soon as wake up, jot down any memories and first thoughts. You can also scribble vague words in the middle of the night if you wake up.

Chapter 16

WHAT KIND OF GIRLFRIEND WILL YOU BE?

OK, you've finally snaffled your dream boy, you've had a couple of dates and you've been on your best behaviour. But as you relax into seeing him will you be cold, aloof and disinterested, or will you cling on like a kitten in a flood?

You can use astrology or other divinatory tools to find out what kind of girlfriend you might be, but it will help you understand what you do and why you do things if you simply work through a flow chart.

To find out your girlfriend type, try the quiz overleaf.

START
Is having a boyfriend very important?

NO → Are you a romantic?

YES ↓

Do you cry about being single?

NO → Are you a romantic?

Are you a romantic? NO → Have you got more than one best mate?

YES ↓

Have you flirted with a mate's boy? YES → Do you enjoy one night snogs?

NO ↓

Would you expect flowers and chocs?

NO → Do you go for older boys?

YES ↓

Would you watch him play footie every week?

NO → Can you overlook characteristics that you don't like?

YES ↓

Would you be heartbroken if it ended? NO → Could you forgive him if he snogged another girl?

YES ↓

TYPE A

Could you forgive him if he snogged another girl? YES → **TYPE B**

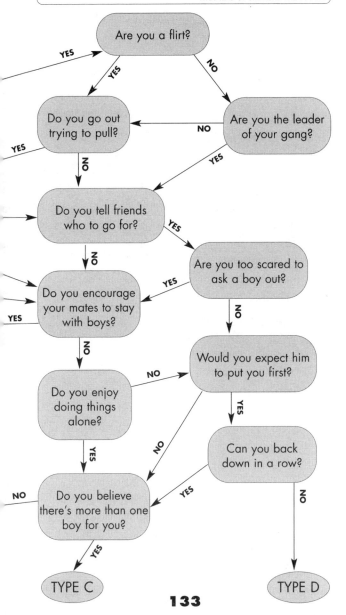

YES → Are you a flirt?

Are you a flirt? — **YES** → Do you go out trying to pull?

Are you a flirt? — **NO** → Are you the leader of your gang?

Are you the leader of your gang? — **NO** → Do you go out trying to pull?

Are you the leader of your gang? — **YES** → Do you tell friends who to go for?

Do you go out trying to pull? — **YES**

Do you go out trying to pull? — **NO** → Do you tell friends who to go for?

Do you tell friends who to go for? — **YES** → Are you too scared to ask a boy out?

Do you tell friends who to go for? — **NO** → Do you encourage your mates to stay with boys?

Are you too scared to ask a boy out? — **YES** → Do you encourage your mates to stay with boys?

Are you too scared to ask a boy out? — **NO** → Would you expect him to put you first?

Do you encourage your mates to stay with boys? — **YES**

Do you encourage your mates to stay with boys? — **NO** → Do you enjoy doing things alone?

Do you enjoy doing things alone? — **NO** → Would you expect him to put you first?

Do you enjoy doing things alone? — **YES** → Do you believe there's more than one boy for you?

Would you expect him to put you first? — **YES** → Can you back down in a row?

Would you expect him to put you first? — **NO** → Do you believe there's more than one boy for you?

Can you back down in a row? — **YES** → Do you believe there's more than one boy for you?

Can you back down in a row? — **NO** → TYPE D

Do you believe there's more than one boy for you? — **NO**

Do you believe there's more than one boy for you? — **YES** → TYPE C

TYPE C

TYPE D

TYPE A – The clinger

You're a big romantic, you love love and want nothing more than to spend every moment with the boy of your dreams. If you found the right boy for you, or even one that would just do, you'd grab him and hang on for dear life. You're the type of girlfriend who boys love and hate. They feel really secure and adored, but they also feel suffocated. Unlike you, they realise that everyone needs to spend time with more than one person. As clingy as you are, you take love seriously, so if you were with a boy who messed you around, you wouldn't stand for it.

Keep your love strong tip: Release your tight grip every now and then.

TYPE B – The pleaser

In relationships you always put him first. You're a romantic, but you're a bit cynical about love because you expect to be hurt. You won't get what you want from your boyfriend, and that won't be his fault it'll be yours. You're giving by nature, but in a relationship you have to take too. Boys aren't bright enough to realise they're being selfish unless you tell them what you want.

Keep your love strong tip: Choose the movie that you want to see. He'll find you more attractive for it.

TYPE C – The free spirit

You don't believe in settling down young, you'd sooner go out with lots of boys until you're really ready to commit to the boy of your dreams. At the moment you're happy to spend your time with friends, you know that they'll always be there for you whereas boys can be fickle. You're incredibly independent and don't believe that you need a boy for anything, which is why lots will be attracted to you. You see the whole dating game as fun and think there's nothing better than a great girly night out, with a brief snog for excitement.

Keep your love strong tip: If someone amazing comes along, don't say no, just because you promised yourself you'd be single.

TYPE D – The dominator

You want your long-term love, but only on your terms. When you find your boy, you'll make him realise that if he's going to be with you, he'd better commit. You're very good at knowing what you want in life, and putting your foot down. When you enter a relationship, you'll do exactly the same. Boys think girls are more complicated than quantum physics, so you're the type of girl who's a relief for them. You tell them what you expect, deserve and want, however you also tell them how to dress, act and behave. That's where you let yourself down.

Keep your love strong tip: Let him be in charge for a while, otherwise you'll never know if he's with you because he likes you or because he's scared of you.

A tip for Goddesses of Wild

Don't alter your ways for a boy. They want the person they fell for. As the relationship changes stay true to yourself.

Chapter 17

MAKE HIM YOURS!

Love Spells

By now, you should have a much clearer idea about who Mr Right is going to be. All you have to do now is go and get him! No, really, pulling boys isn't nearly as hard as we make out. There are two great techniques you can use to bag him and they both use your own Goddess powers.

What are love spells?
Love spells are very simple, innocent charms that you can carry out, alone or with a mate, to help push that boy a little nearer to you.

How do they work?
They vary from spell to spell, but all white witch spells are innocent and fun. They take into consideration the problem you're having, and try to work a remedy. They never ever use spells to hurt or revenge someone, as proper white witches believe bad spells come back on you twofold.

What can they tell you about yourself?
Spells aren't really about self-analysis, but the fact that you're deciding to put the effort into casting a spell tells you that you must be quite into him!

BEWITCH THAT BOY!
Why aren't you two a happy couple yet? Check out the problem and find the right spell for you.

Spell for the boy who's being aloof and not romantic
Pour some sugar into a small cup or bowl and take it up to your bedroom. Write his name on a piece of paper, fold up the paper, and bury it in the sugar. Leave it there for a week. By then you should have managed to sweeten him up!

Spell for the boy who seems to be interested

Get two short pieces of string and knot them together. Carry it around with you, in your school bag or purse for a few days. Then drop it somewhere relevant to him, it could be under his desk, outside his house, on his footie pitch, anywhere. Be discreet – he doesn't have to notice it to help the bonding process.

Spell for the boy you've fallen out with

Find something small that reminds you of him. It could be anything from a picture of his favourite rugby team to a poem he's written for you. Put it into an envelope and put it into the freezer overnight to cool him down.

Spell for the boy who doesn't know you exist

Find a photo of yourself on your own, put it on the floor and walk around it. Circle the photo three times chanting, 'Go from here into your head.' This should get him thinking about you. Be careful not to use a photo with one of your friends in – you don't want to magic the two of them together!

Spell for the boy who is too shy to talk to you

Tear a piece of paper into four. On each piece write one word that makes you think of him. Put the pieces of paper under your pillow overnight. The following day go out of your way to say hello, and hopefully he'll have found some words to say back to you.

Use your body!

If you've cast your magic, and you're not seeing any immediate results, it's time to take action!

There are two things you can do to let him know you're interested at this point. You could walk up to him, say, 'So how about a date on Saturday night?' then plant a big smacker on his lips. Or, if you're not feeling brave enough for the first option, you can use your body language.

As a girl and a Goddess, you have endless power in communication: even the way you flick your hair can have a message! Getting a boy to notice you, and realise you're interested, is easy. Just follow these simple steps that you can use in just one day or evening.

EIGHT STEPS TO SUCCESS

1 When you walk into the room, check out where he is, then walk to a spot where you know he can see you.

2 Next, look around everywhere, as if you're looking for someone. After about a minute, check your watch and walk out, as if the person you're trying to find hasn't arrived yet. This will make him notice you and intrigue him.

3 After at least ten minutes go back into the room. This time acknowledge him. Look him straight in the eye and smile. This will show him that you're friendly and that you've noticed him.

4 After a while find a way to sit near him. Point your knees and upper body in his direction. This says that you're interested in talking to him. If you can't sit, lean against a wall, directing your body his way.

5 Find a reason to get talking to him, even if it's an obvious, 'Oh, sorry I bumped into you.' Don't be panicked – chat about the party, or whatever event you're at. At this point what your mouth is saying isn't important, it's what your body's saying that counts. Don't cross your arms,

141

instead look relaxed and lean back slightly. This tells him that you're open to getting to know him.

6 If you're getting on OK, gently tuck your hair behind your ear with your hand. This is just a flirty little sign that spells out that you want to look attractive to him.

7 Find an excuse to touch him! Either offer to go and get him a Coke and touch him on the arm as you say, 'I'll be back in a moment.' Or brush past him. This slight physical contact lets him know that you're feeling comfortable with him, and are so relaxed that if he asked you out, you'd more than likely say yes.

8 At all times when you two are chatting, keep your eyes fixed on his and face your body directly at him.

By now you've shouted 'I'm interested!', but is he? First read his body language too, but with boys, there are other super obvious signs that shout 'I'm into you too!'